PHOENIX RISING

PHOENIX RISING

Onward and Upward

SAMANTHA PRASAD

ISBN: 0692541225
ISBN 13: 9780692541227

For the dream catchers,
Icarian birds,
fantasy keepers,
astrology nerds –

the hopeless romantics
and storytelling fanatics,
the monster slayers, fierce fighters,
and all of my phoenix flyers.

INTRODUCTION

I have always been fascinated with words. The flow of language – romantic, stuttered, or otherwise. I can't pinpoint exactly what prompted the attraction, but it has been a lifelong relationship. I find magic in prose, and literature has filled my spirit with yearning, learning, and a raw sense of wonder. Words led to reading, and reading led to writing, and writing led to living out a dream. A dream you now hold in your hands. Truly, thank you.

Regardless of your reasons for purchasing this book, I hope you find words that you can relate to throughout it. It is literature that has gotten me through some of my darkest days, and I hope at least one of you can find solace in a piece of prose or poetry that is hidden in the following pages.

While I have always loved to write, poetry is something that graced me only over the last few years. I feel incredibly lucky to share my work with you. I hope you take each piece in and feel as much as I put into it – my heart, tears, bits and pieces of my soul. Don't be afraid to take your time reading it – my book may best be read on a lazy, hammock-swinging kind of day. Where you feel like the world hasn't quite given up on us. I hope you get to know me better. I hope you get to know yourself better. But most of all, I hope you enjoy this. And thank you for joining one woman's dream to build a world of words.

Laugh vibrantly. Live graciously. Love fiercely.

Always,
Sam

ABOUT ME

Maybe I should start by letting you get to know me.
After all, I struggle with letting people in.
But I also aim to bear sunlight on my shortcomings,
and hopefully burn them off like the end of a candlewick.
My favorite color is blue, like the eyes I always wished I had.
(Maybe that explains my taste in men.)
I have read *Wuthering Heights* at least four times a year since
high school.
It was Emily Brontë's only novel, and with one try, she managed
to write a classic. And there is something so tragic about
Heathcliff and Catherine's love affair that I can't help but
live amongst the brokenhearted.
I fall in love way too fast and far too easily, but the loves
I have had tend to last.
They stay with me long after hundreds of suns fade and
into the lowest octaves of echoed memories.
I used to pretend I could be one of the Power Rangers
when I grew up, because fixing people was an addiction
even at five years old.
I do my best thinking when I am traveling,
soaring off of seawashed cliffs and bathing in foreign sands.
I can't stand the taste of coffee, but lose myself in its scent.
The best way to my heart is through my head –
enthrall me with literature and music and if you let me

in enough to become my muse, you'll have me forever.
I believe in ghosts, in time travel, and in a life after death.
I am still afraid of the dark, but after living in such dark
times for years, I have learned that facing your fears is
truly the only way to shed light on what you can overcome.
I love cherries in the summertime and have never been
partial to wine, I prefer the high that I get whenever I ponder
the cosmos and this firecracker universe that we all set ablaze.
I whistle with the blue jays, and I still want to photograph
packs of wild mustangs somewhere out on open land.
I am sarcastic and sassy, and while I am terrified of heights,
I wish I could fly.
I dance constantly, like a tribe of one around moonlit bonfires.
But mostly, I am always seeking change, to surround myself
with others that can only better me and to sleep with prose
that will inspire me to write something that will make at least
one person out there feel safe. Feel warm. Feel understood.

STRAY SHOPPING CART

My heart is rather lonely at times.
I passed a stray shopping cart stuck
somewhere in suburbia.
Under a bare branched tree with its
limbs tapping on the windows of a
house of limestone and copper.
Out of sight, out of mind.
And all out of place.

Tissues stretched over one too many
times, canvasing out of business car
washes and shoe stores, looking for
company on a cemented stretch of land.
I think I will wait for the fog to lift;
I think I will store my heart in that
shopping cart, and wait for it to start
beating again.

PAPA'S HOUSE

Grandfather's - to me he has always been more fondly known as Papa - house always smelled of pancake batter. Pancakes and orange and vanilla musk from his aftershave. The warm haze of the stove's steam left me an eager five-year-old, awaiting the sound of the spatula's spin and the sizzle of butter and cooking oil. Nothing else could beat the privilege he always gave me of topping each pancake with six chocolate chips. In all of his cooking perfection, he always managed to maintain the texture of the chocolate, so that the chips would melt on my tongue rather than in the cushion of pan-heated batter.

And then he would sit. A pile of three pancakes atop a plastic plate, with Aladdin and Jasmine grinning up at me, and a glass of two percent milk that would wash away the excess chocolate smeared on my lips. My feet barely grazed the kitchen floor, dangling and kicking Papa against his right shin as he retrieved his favorite deck of playing cards from across the table. *Solitaire, Sam,* he would relay to me as he split the deck up into miniature piles. I was always in awe of how he could win every time. I would come to realize that in his frustration he would merely scoop the cards back up and start over, only giving my naïve self the illusion that he continuously won. He had the advantage that I did not learn how to properly play the game until I was eight years old.

The cards, worn and weathered, much like the hands that dealt them, held the story of a thoughtful and precise man that was calculating in everything he did. Which can only explain his precision with those pancakes. I never understood his fascination with those cards until I was far older. Until I understood him as a man that valued stability and those calm and quiet moments that can only be found in a pile of dishes left untouched, sunlight strewn curtains, and 52 pieces of waxed, cardboard paper. Stability and some form of escape from those dirty dishes and the leftover melted butter that would crust along the stove's burners.

Even in my cotton candy pink pajamas and tangled web of dark hair, I knew that I wanted to be like him. You know how in grade school, you're always required to write about a "hero" of yours, and all the saps alike - including myself - would pick a family member. He was unfailingly mine. After solitaire, he would put on a record. The same one he played day after day. I may have only been five, but I adored this song. *Unchained Melody* by The Righteous Brothers. The harmony would oscillate through the hallway, the percussion would lightly thump against the walls, and then I would hear him sing. *I need your love, God speed your love to me...* The familiar voice that knew every lyric, every fluctuating tone, and he could sing just as well - if not better - than those Righteous Brothers. Just add that to the list of many reasons why I have always aspired to be like him. For I can barely hold a note to save my life. But just like my grandfather, I knew every word by heart. I still do. I would spin around, my toes indenting the carpet, slow dancing to The Righteous Brothers featuring Narciso Mostasisa.

Three minutes, the music would begin to fade, and like clockwork, Papa would reach into his shirt pocket and pull out a honey-colored handkerchief. I would notice him dab at the corners of his eyes, mini crystals of salt sinking into the handsome lines of his face. *Allergies, Sam,* he said to me in a reassuring tone. I could hear the scratch of the record player's needle as it called out to someone to cease its itching ways, and though there was silence, this was not one of our calm and quiet moments. For I could not understand why tears would make a home in such a wonderful man's eyes.

He would take my hand, it seemed so small in his palm, and whirl me around. My long hair would catch against his arm, and I could see another crease in his face. A soft smile that matched his gentle eyes. The handkerchief found its way back into his shirt pocket, and he would continue to hum our song. *Lonely rivers flow, to the sea, to the sea...* He hummed it just for me - my five-year-old self felt so honored. And like many other things, I would eventually realize he was humming it for her, too. In hopes she was listening.

The sun rose over the sky, baking the living room, where Papa and I sat and watched old Western films. *The Alamo* was on AMC again, and Papa knew how much I loved the horses, it was one of the many reasons I would sit against his hip on the plastic-laden couch while we waited for lunchtime to beckon. *That's John Wayne, Sam,* he told me. And although I was lost in the plotlines of *True Grit* and *Sands of Iwo Jima,* I had the best companion for company. A man that would even leave his favorite films behind when I would scurry away whenever a horse was shot. As with everything else, his reassurance that *no horsies were actually hurt* calmed me. I would smush my cheeks into the warmth of his chest and once more, I inhaled the vanilla and orange that proved to be the most familiar scent I can identify with to this day.

Back in the kitchen, Papa would make his famous chicken adobo, but over the last year, I noticed that one thing was always missing from our lunch dishes: rolls of lumpia. That was her job, after all. And I hadn't had those since last summer. I missed them. Papa missed her.

Once again, he was quiet as he chewed his chicken. I stirred mine into my rice. My meals were always so disproportionate - far more rice than protein. I had a feeling Papa felt a little disproportionate, too. I did my best to equal whatever was missing; but I think I fell a little short. Figuratively and literally.

I wandered down the hall after lunch, my belly full, into Papa's bedroom. There sat his cologne, and next to it, a half-empty bottle of her perfume. Along with her bath salts and still in the closet were her lace nightgowns that she had always let me wear even though they were ten sizes too big for me. I would parade down that hall as if I were a princess. And Papa had always treated me like such. Through all of my sashays and twirls, he would applaud, and that honey-colored handkerchief would always remain seated in his pocket. Now whenever I tried to amuse him, the handkerchief would always make a guest appearance. Once again, at the corner of his eyes. Stable, calm, quiet - strong. That's how he wanted me to see him. That's what he wanted to be. That's what she made him.

He placed the record on the player once more. The final time for today. Two times and that would be all. And so I adorned a lace nightgown, spun down the hallway, and the lyrical tune went. This was our tradition. Mine and Papa's. For the last year. *All alone I gaze at the stars, at the stars, dreaming of my love far away...* I heard him sing. And then I noticed him out of the corner of my eye. By their dresser. He was softly touching the outline of a frame, the glass that held their wedding picture. She was adorned in white lace; he was looking studly in his tuxedo. And he seemed so happy. The creases by his eyes, while not permanent back then, lit up his face. A wide smile that matched his brown eyes. Full of hope for the future. Full of hope for the woman beside him. *Has it really only been a year?* I heard him whisper to the picture. To her. *And time goes by so slowly,* the record played.

His face reflected against the portrait. His well-worn face alongside her youthful one. A drop of water slid down the glass, tracing the bodice of her dress and settling into the left corner of the frame. And just this once, Papa couldn't reach his handkerchief in time.

LEFTOVER GHOSTS

She haunted me, that little girl.
Flying paper kites and feeding
those hungry ducks that invaded the koi pond.
Sipping Capri Sun from mason jars
and candy cane straws.
Licking snow from cedar branches,
and feeding the lions at the zoo.

I see her everywhere.
In the sunlit particles that dance,
in the air like pixies coming home.
In the scarlet petals that
seek shade under the willows.
In my own eyes that cannot deny
the broken childhood from whence she came.
She may be a figment, but still, a tattered ghost.
Carefree, innocent, four years old.
In a pink dress and flushed cheeks.
I wonder whom she might have been,
where she might have been now.
Oh stolen innocence, I wish I could have
known what she would have left behind.

CANDY WRAPPER HEART

Sometimes I don't think I know much about anything. I sprout ideas from crinkled candy wrappers and stale muffin tops with teeth marks here and there. On the wrappers, not the muffins. Probably because my dog got to them. I guess I shouldn't leave the kitchen such a mess. Pots, pans, a stray oven mitt.

But then again, that's me. Messy. Frazzled. Scattered. A windstorm kind of disaster. But there's enough of me to go around. I've strewn so many pieces of myself all over this town. Dotted cityscapes and Hollywood lettering landmarks. I break hearts while I keep mine hidden under the bed. Or maybe I left it under the coasters that once shallowed the tide of condensation from that glass of whiskey. You know, the one that's still sitting in the kitchen sink. Probably amongst the grimy pots and pasta sauce pans.

No wonder my heart is nowhere to be found.

CRUSHED STARS

They need a new word for the kind of hurt he created.

He spun evil out of breathless virtue and stole the purity of angels.

Destroyed space bound dreams and crushed the stars until they could shine no more.

He lived in darkness, organizing lit jars of organs and freeing the monsters of the night.

There is no fiery bond, no familial connection.

Not with the man that stole so much and preyed on the young.

I will dispose of him at all ends of the earth, and cling to the leftovers of a damaged soul.

It happened far too fast and far too soon.

And it was completely out of my control.

Karma slumbered through my childhood, but once it finds his bed, she won't be so quick to leave when the morning comes.

MISPLACED FAITH

It is 12:56 p.m. I am standing in the middle of a chapel. And I have no idea how the fuck I got here. Shit, did I black out...again?

Which reminds me, I probably shouldn't swear in a church. Hell, I probably shouldn't even be *in* a church. It's been three years – and even longer than that since my last confession.

My face is tear streaked, and I feel stupid for being this hysterical in front of God and the statue of Jesus staring back at me. A woman enters. "Honey, if you are pregnant, have the baby."

Well, even if this woman is judging me, at least God isn't. I hope.
But I'm definitely not pregnant. I'm praying.
Praying to remember what brought me here, and praying to forget what drove me here.

ROCK BOTTOM

"Imagine two pillars of a building. What happens when one of the pillars is suddenly taken away? The building crumbles. You are the building, Sam. And one of your supporting pillars has, unfortunately, been stripped away."

I sat there quietly, tears pooling. I hated feeling like this. I hated admitting when my therapist was right. Hell, I hated admitting when anyone other than me was right.

"Stubbornness. It runs in your family." Damn it, he had gotten that right, too.

"It hurts to miss someone every second. On top of everything else," I told him, reaching for the pile of tissues that sat like a small cloud in my lap. Much better than the one hanging over me.

I saw him grab the little white pad, the Rx logo in bold, black script. "I'm going to write you a prescription for an antidepressant. Just something short term."

I sighed. So this is what the bottom feels like.

JOLTED DOVES

She questioned why things happened the way they did.
Crouched on two legs, wings clipped, she knelt among the rubble of her past.

"Why?"

"My darling, you are a phoenix. The flames that burn you are the ones that will set you free. Don't you see how they tremble in your stead? Jolted doves and sacred blue heat that know of your divinity. You are meant to rise from the ashes, not remain buried by them."

KNOW SOMETHING

Know something –
when you are down on prayerful knees,
feeling so unsure,
gazing out at those small sailboats,
floating in a sea of glamour.

Wishing you could cast your anchor
to another galaxy,
know something –
you are not just another casualty.

You will discover a guiding lighthouse,
one that is medieval, metallic, and motherly.
It will ease your sorrows and suffering,
swab away your agony.

When your head is awash in sadness,
and the tide is far too violent to tread,
Recall the strength of your own heart
to keep you in her stead.

If you are standing over the bluff,
feeling so unsure,
wanting to fall, to jump, to end the suffering,
remember this –
you have always been more than enough.

PAPER AIRPLANES

There once was an old rooftop,
littered with moss and parched leaves,
where we would sit and fold paper airplanes.
We launched them every day at 4 p.m.,
just as the sun began to dip.
I knew you were hoping they would reach
heights our chubby hands were not yet ready for.
I saw them drift past the cathedral,
heard the bells toll for the daily 4:30 mass,
and thought that since we were higher than
that carmine brick church,
we must somehow be closer to God.
Two happy hearts, living in scuff-soled
shoes atop our one-mile radius world.

And then God called you,
higher than the cathedral,
higher than our rooftop,
and now there is no place for us.
I cried that I would follow you anywhere.
Because overnight,
I knew somehow we were ready.
We had the whole world before our feet.
(L i t e r a l l y).

Yet here I sit now,
twirling leaves and picking at moss.
One lonely heart,
one scuffed soul.

PHOENIX RISING

I watch my paper airplanes cast
shadows against the dipping sun,
hoping they will reach new heights,
hoping they will make their way to you,
and hoping heaven sends one down for me, too.

LIMITLESS

Remember how we used to go to
the fairgrounds every summer?
The carousel was far too crowded,
so we opted for the Ferris wheel.

Where you helped me conquer my fear of heights.

I looked down and everything
and everyone looked so small –
even the cotton candy looked like
shrunken clouds of pink and blue.
And you would swing the carriage
back and forth just to hear me laugh.

Or scream. Usually both.

We always purchased those wristbands.
You know the ones that granted you
unlimited access to all of the rides?
We hated carrying tokens around –
not so much because of the pocket jingle,
but because we never wanted anything
extra to weigh us down.

But that's how I used to think love was. Unlimited.

The kind that gives you skyscraper-sized butterflies,
just like the kind we used to get right
before we boarded the Gravitron.

Around and around we would spin.
The Hurricane took us into the calm of the storm.
And I knew I could hang upside down
in those Starships with you forever.

    Until my head burst. Or my heart.

My heart was far more likely to give in first.
And then I thought maybe you could
see how much love would spill out for you.

    Unlimited.

THE MAD SCIENTIST

I want to know you better.
Pick apart your mind like a
science experiment gone right.
Hypothesize about our future.
Prove theories of the existence
of angels behind your eyes.
Fall down the tunnel of your soul
like a penicillin accident.

Discover the curves of your ears
and the knots of your wrist.
Wire them together with the
architecture of a time machine.
The kind of delicacy that requires
precise hands and a decisive heart.
Let me concoct potions with your words
and write novels of your most random
laughs and your darkest days of thought.
For you may think yourself insane,
but it is I that is mad for you.

OLIVER

Let me tell you what I love about you.
Let me sing you an ode.
Tell you I'm lucky.
Lucky that I wake up to you.
I love that you smell like coffee and
incense and that we wake up with
cat fur in our hair.
That you only need five minutes to get
ready and you feel like everything I
have been waiting for.
I love that you pray, and that you
pray with me.
And that you pray **for** me.
That you laugh at my jokes and
eat dinner with my folks.
You read books I recommend and
eat pizza at 3 a.m.
You know how to kiss and make love
and keep me on my toes.
You challenge me;
you're my best friend.
You are an expert at impressions and
call me sweets.

I love that you still remind me about that
strip poker game I lost, and that I
still owe you new sheets.
You feel like everything I know and
everything I want.

So come what may,
with you is where I'll stay.

CLIFFSIDE

I remember thinking we had missed the turn to his house.
I missed that same turn the first time I tried to find his place.
Only tonight I wasn't driving.
Instead of veering right, the car remained straight,
and I had no idea where we were headed.

Jitterbugs danced in my stomach;
a surprise played along the corners of his eyes.
Spoiled or not, I wanted to know him.
I *want* to know him.
The soul of him, the halves, every piece.

Somewhere at land's end, I saw his brilliance.
The sun tickled the fringes of the clouds.
Exquisite rays that decorated the power lines
with Easter pastels and July candlelight.

Forehead kisses, sideways glances,
looking out over a sea of diamonds,
the west sweating off its day,
seamless rainbows of gospel hues.
Pegasus swimming the sea sky,
where we opened our mouths to
steal drops of Jupiter.

Under shades of blue,
the world flipped upside down,
and the mountains touched both the clouds and sea.
Lit with cotton ball wisps and awakening moonbeams.

PHOENIX RISING

The ocean shimmered against the fading light,
reflecting the Pacifica cliffs,
ebbing in and out of secret beaches and broken beer bottles.

Amongst the moors, I was spellbound.
Bewitched. Breathtakingly bold.
My heart flowed like a gold rush,
so open, yet so full for him.

Fallen rocks, colliding souls,
Post-It proverbs collected on scrolls,
That night we made love to certainty.
At the edge of forever, I fell into eternity.

MOON CRATERS
& STARDUST

That night you took me to the cliffs,
you whispered into the dying sun and
shook the hollows of my bones;
dense secrets that my heart lapped up
like honeydew and cantaloupe juice.

Your hands wandered the caves of
my spine and the branches of my hair.
You left me breathless; a dissolving
poetess, melted by a foreign tongue
of love and lust, and you lapped me up
from moon craters and stardust.

WE ARE

I believe that even in our stillest moments, we have creativity flowing through our veins.

Like deep rivers that feed into the souls of crashing waves and sea salt reefs.

Each of us has our own version of poetry.

Our spirits remain curious long after our palms wrinkle and branches of jasmine make their way into the corners of furrowed pages.

We own the way we see the world – we mold ourselves from carmine clay and wind brushed balconies.

There are days where my mind stills – where I peel the bark off of trees just to feel the sap between my fingers. Sticky grains that nurture the roots that run beneath my callused feet.

My hands shape sand castles and carve jack-o-lanterns in June, purely to milk the breast of productivity.

And yet, we cannot hold ourselves to such a standard.

We must not always do what we are told.

We must find passion in the necessity of life.

Like building beanbag towers and blanket covered forts.

We can find our childlike hearts in down comforters and Silverstein manuscripts.

Whatever we do, we make.

We feed our rivers with diamond droplets and tie dyed hairstyles.

With our limbs, we sculpt.

With our toes, we paint scripture in the soil.

And with every breath we exhale, we live out our art.

DESERT GODDESS

I am a desert goddess,
clothed in golden sands and carafes of stardust.
I kiss the skies and follow my naked feet
to the oasis streams.
Cacti come alive, their arms plunging toward
the heavens; thorns piercing the wild air.

Here I listen to the howl of coyotes,
arched coats pointed toward the moon's window.
A melancholy sound of crimson and wine.
My salted skin tastes of sweat and
South American chilies.
Fire and gunpowder;
a combustion as bright as the constellations.

Here I live in uncivilization,
painting graffiti across porous rocks of jade
and withering riverbeds.
I tiptoe past roadrunners and shroud myself
in an Egyptian night.
Somewhere to the east I hear the coo of
the Red Sea lapping up the Mediterranean.

It is in this place of enchantment,
stooped in the histories of so many deities before,
that I live and breathe again.
And I learn it all over, day in, day out,
in this paradise where curiosity never dies.

GOLDEN CLOCKS & EVENING TRAINS

The summer heat is sticky tonight.
It coats us in honey and Himalayan salt.
The world moves slowly.
Golden clocks
     and
     evening trains
churn through fields of foxtails and blue shamrocks.
Fireflies dwell on clouds and
fairy bells lay in the woodlands.
We fill mason jars with ice and lemonade
and two sips of whiskey.
Sugar spun lace and cobwebs of moonlight.
The porch swing rocks lovers' feet
to sleep and bonfires decorate July shores.
We dance in tribes.

Naked arms and legs,
bathing in Gobi Desert sands
and collecting volcanic glass.
We build shaded forts from Egyptian cotton
and sleep under the stars.
Children camping among the dunes of coral.
The sun gives way to a milky moon and
we count sheep until the chimes of midnight.

DAYDREAM

It was a Friday – the day we met.

An ordinary day in June.

That winding staircase swept the darkness of my dress away,

and the way you met my eyes – it was transcendent.

We built our love to float on clouds.

We wandered the San Francisco streets, across that golden bridge, and touched the fog as it lay to sleep with the bay.

Strolled through farmer's markets on that Sunday, picking tangerines and pomegranates, homemade pasta and chopping basil leaves for our pesto sauce that we never got quite right.

And then we chased stars through rainstorms and you kissed me without an umbrella, and the rest of my days became extraordinary.

But then your eyes looked away;

I descended that staircase, and without a word, you were gone.

So I guess it is time to let you go;

To and fro, to and fro.

I will keep my daydreams hidden behind the fog that hung so low.

THE KEY

I will *kiss* down the sinuous lines of your neck,
Trace the veins of the arms that hold me so dear.
I will *follow* the curve of your spine,
To roads far less *traveled*.
I will *know* the secrets that your lips hold,
And *chase* the light behind your eyes.
Surely and sweetly, with the faintest of whispers,
I will *unlock* your heart.

NEXT STEP

I think I've grown enough now to know how to love you back.
Like purple rain and indigo orchids.
In the rawest sunburnt flesh, I will adore every inch of you, creature.
You see, you healed me, scarred and charred and marred.
So I will sing fire alarm songs,
and shower you in sandalwood and orange zest.

You see, I am ready to fall now.
I am prepared to blaze this life through all seasons.
Breaking glass and scattering diamonds through rundown churches and shriveled gardens.
Slow dancing to Frank Sinatra records and Beethoven melodies.
So please, don't drop me just yet,
you see, I am ready to take that next step.

PIER 39

San Francisco wind inscribed Braille on my skin,
but how generous that tiger lily sun was to
contemplate the golden stripes of his hair.
I found myself jealous of her rays,
for I wanted to be the only one to regard him today.

We walked along the pier, felt the unevenness of
maple and rosewood planks, fingertips extended –
a balance beam outstretched –
we salivated at the scent of baking waffle cones.
Like the sun, I could feel his smile on me
just as I could feel her shine.

Two wanderers, we strolled past the carousel of
pirouettes, carved with sea dragons, unicorns,
and spinning chariots of plastic fire.
Through the mirror maze, I heard the cries
of bobbing sea lions, and somewhere
along the promenade, we found our way
through the crowd of Oakley sunglasses and
sombrero-sized beach hats
to barrels of colored sands.

The hues, pigments, aromas –
they glistened through those artisan bottles.
An alchemist's mix, he concocted sandalwood,
Bergamot, and lavender, while I scooped
petals of lilacs onto my palms just so
I could hold hands with the flowers.

Jars of bath salts filled to the brim
with minerals of mint, California breeze,
and vanilla gemstones.
The shades flirted with one another much like
two hands resting in mutual back pockets.
Where we adorned our necks with perfume.
Where we lost ourselves in the barrels of blooms.

THE PROPOSAL

Your car spun out right before the entrance to the I-80.
We needed to go east, not west.
I saw the frustration clouding your eyes.
I looked overhead.
A thunderstorm was making love to the clouds;
I knew the rain would birth soon.
I stood under the awning of that box store,
the one that probably crushed the mom's and the pop's.
Left them to sink into Indian burial grounds.

I tied a knot on my ring finger to make sure I wouldn't forget.
The fire in your eyes the rain would never wash away.
Even in lightning anger, I adored your firestorm passion.
The zest, the spontaneity that came in as fast and
fleeting as unpredictable asteroids.
It burned through everything – your flame.
And so I continued to tie knots:
Bachmann, Bourchier, bowline –
I needed something to hold onto,
when I had to let go of the question I knew you would never ask.

GRAVITY

It was not often I was granted seclusion.
A solitude kept with company of
sparkling condensation and plumes of
smoke from that beach house stove.

I smelled of sage leaves and pineapple cubes,
with a strawberry plant in bloom atop the windowsill.
The waves brought a warm wind, rolling with the
tide like the freckles that ran up my arms.

I knew that, like the tide, I had something
to draw me in. But the moon comes and goes.
It is gravity that remains in bed with sun stained waves.
But pull me hard enough, and that, too, is questionable.

GLORY DAYS

Long live our glory days.
Where we donned captain's hats
and sailed the seas so free,
lingering in the breath after our first kiss,
we learned just how magnetic we could be.
We won wars and crucified our love
upon golden strings of the sun.
So uncomplicated, we flowed through
open windows and doors –

It was seamless.
And the knots we tied birthed butterflies
and silk ribbons in our hair.
We held each other like anchors to our bodied ships.
Had I known it was merely a phase,
I would have stayed in them far more,

long
live
our
glory
days.

OUT TO SEA

My love, you are my lighthouse.
I promise to remain yours,
let your glow lead me to the shore.
Away from the mayhem,
away from the chaos,
out to sea, to the foam,
where the waves lap to a
harmony that is all our own.

SILLY STRING SUMMERS

Under the neon lights,
beneath the pale moon,
we shared pop rocks that dissolved
like shooting stars between our lips.
A sugary, sweet kind of carbonation,
we fought our way back from
tangled power lines and blackout summers.
We decorated our backyards in
silly string and spilled paint cans.
Lived in moon bounce houses,
and bathed in the effervescence of our youth.
Our love soared above the heavens,
and floated like inflatable castles in the sky.
High off of candied kisses and flashlight fireflies.

LOVES ME NOT

Sometimes you wonder about me.
You think about what our life would be like now.
In star shaped formations and graffiti rooftops.
You wonder if we are daring and brave enough
to leave our superhero capes strung on hangers
and light finger held firecrackers.

You go back to the moment we met.
I am in a flowing dress of aquamarine fire and
you predict forever within the first month
when you hear about my love for poetry,
literature, and dead writers.

How we led the dark of night into golden sunrises
and let Lucky Charms melt on our tongues
as the stars slept.
Sometimes you wonder about me.

My God, I hope you do.

CHECKMATE

He looked like royalty.
Polished, clean, pressed collars
and white gold pocket watches.
He was not arrogant like the kings
of history, but he bestowed
favor on me.

I never really knew why.

I did know this:

I'm not very proper
(I like to fuck and say fuck),
I'm indecently imperfect,
and my wrists are decorated
with gaudy gems rather
than genuine ones.

As much as I longed to be
his queen, I never could be.

I am a pawn – a rook maybe –
but sooner more often than later,
I will be r e p l a c e d.

PATCHWORK CLOUDS

There is a soft rumble as snow across the sky descends.
Patchwork from a quilt of clouds that beckons time to stand still.
They rise like morning doves before the cinnamon sun,
before the creatures of the universe stretch their limbs
across dew droplets and rose petal sheets.
Beads of champagne light waltz with falling leaves
of primrose and wind struck feathers fallen from gumdrop trees.

    The giants remain in their caves;
    the mermaids reside in their oceanic cove.

They cover the earth from asteroids, comets,
and put shooting stars to bed.
Tracing cigarette smoke along the horizon, they exhale
like breaths on a winter morning, and fill our lungs with
yesterday's ashes and the promise of a new day.

FANTASY

On a turbulent day such as this one,
I let myself dawdle in my surreptitious fantasies.
They uncoil in the synapses of my lustful brain
like tumbleweeds caught in a sandstorm.
I find myself dancing around carmine flames
beside the fire pits strewn along starlit sands,
and singing your name to an ultraviolet moon.

Darling, you see, your love has driven me quite mad,
but I cannot help entangle myself in my muse.
I want to live with you in fields of sugarcane and
unkempt flowers, where this universe of fire and ice
can leave us uninterrupted in our bed of leaves and dew.
I can only hope to pass through the summers and
springs with you, sipping on sweet tea and apricot seeds.

Yes, it is only through my mind that I can live out
this life with you. And what wild things we are.
Roaming the streets of Paris and the hills of Tuscany,
only to get lost in our universe of dreams.
Here is where we grow ivory orchids and spread
our toes on the edge of everything that is holy and fertile.

With you I stretch free from the hands of Fate;
I can arch my back and be swept away in the poetry
of your voice and the winds brushed with
rumors of a timeless love.
I can paint the whiskey on your breath and distill
myself in the vapors of your whispered breaths.

Because my fantasies, love, they nourish me.
With eyes closed and my lungs filled,
I breathe in every satisfaction that you offer.
Everything between us that remains unborn,
that is kept in such a colorful grey matter.
On a turbulent day such as this one,
I carve our initials into old tree trunks;
I catch myself inhaling a heliotrope afterglow,
and I count the days of our lives on my knuckle lines,
each indent a dream my marrow stows.

FOUR-FOOT INFINITIES

Last night I witnessed a pocket watch sky.
With every passing headlight, the hands of time
led me back to my childhood.
Clouds of cotton candy swirls.
Sticks of spun sugar that my lips longed to taste.
Bonbon stars and a confectionary moon.

There is an inexplicable bravery that comes
with being young and trivial.
We never had to explain why capes let us
believe we could fly, and why we
befriended dragons and knew things of lore and legend.
I wanted to soar like Icarus – sing like a phoenix –
and let my inhibitions fall like loose feathers come
undone from the honey, syrup, and wax.

I let the setting sun linger on my tongue, tasting
remnants of pop rock asteroids and lollipop trees.
And on days when we can no longer see the stars,
I will think back to this moment –
recall how colorful we were –
lionhearted kids that used to paint chalk rainbows
on dancing sidewalks.

We knew what freedom was,
understood how to tap maple and music from
the trees, play jazz with only our hands and thighs,
and whistle with our lips upon blades of grass.
How I wish we could be mavericks now.

Gazing out of my window, the sky seemed never ending.
Just like the rainbows, the chalk, and our fingers
smeared with stardust, we never imagined the chapter of
those days would end.

Our eyes were charged with curiosity, our fingers inquisitive.
We wanted to know all – we wanted to be all.
Making heaven out of star-like fireflies.
We were four-foot infinities.
We were boundless. Just like the sky.

THE NEXT LEFT

We were just young teenagers,
looking for misadventures and
any way to satiate our curious hands.

I would ride on the handles
of your bicycle,
the wheels tracing through every
streetlamp lit puddle on that
still October night.

The clearness of the sky
mimicked the way we used to
see the future.
We knew exactly where we
were going, even if it was just
me telling you to take the next left.

You'd turn, the autumn air
caressing my face, and I would look
back at you, your smile
dusted with candy corn gold,
my tongue stained
jolly rancher pink.

Crystals in our mouths,
crystals in our eyes –
we were young,
but we were so, so free.

ADVENTURE

That afternoon we let adventure marinate in our bones.
"Let's just drive until we run out of road."
What lay before us was only a mere separation of land and sky.

The heavens' ocean splashed waves of white foam.
Cotton ball clouds soaked up the niagara of a sky
fastened with sapphire and indigo.
Daisies and daffodils leapt in spontaneous patches
nestled in sage pastures.
Eyes of dwarf owls gazed at us behind
tilted picket fences.

An oxidized mailbox sprouted vines of jasmine
and strawberry blossoms, for even rusting metal
can provide a beautiful haven for whimsical wildlife.
Grizzled, gray-haired porches played bluegrass
and country music. My ribs harmonized
banjo twangs and harp strings.

Until the gravel turns to sand.
Until the sky turns to sea.
Until dirt ceases to settle in the crevices
of our eyelids and we feel the longing kiss
of salt against our lips.
Where sienna land ends, where jade ocean begins.
Where our feet can turn to flippers and sirens sing
and mermaids beckon and I can finally say,
"Baby, we made it."

EXPOSURE

It really is something –
when you meet someone that exposes
you to new things.
Unheard of things.
He shared his angels and demons so mine
finally had others to play with,
and they could let me (us) be.
His sketches of dark musings
with purple eyes and magnolia locks;

he intimidated me,
but he never frightened me.
He had the power to fold the sun in half
and shake the moon until it peppered
the universe with sapphires and opals.
His voice surrounded me like a magnetic field –
I was constantly drawn to him
without ever meaning to be.
I wanted to learn everything he knew.
I wanted to read him slow,
like a classic novel – turning page by page,
highlighting the prose that sounds
more beautiful than anything I could ever write.

Like chasing butterflies in a thunderstorm.
Memorize every sinew, every crevice,
see the stars on his skin and
create poetry in our lovemaking.
He has a soul as deep as the ocean,
and I welcomed drowning,
so long as I could call him mine.

BREAKFAST IN BED

I quite like the smell of your bed sheets,
pairs of toes and fingers laced in silk.
Emerald crystals of playful tenderness;
they sweep me up into a mouthful of whispers.

A hallway filled with tiptoes and draping light,
with your voice, coated in velvet and honey.
Naked skin remains untouched, static cling hangs
in the air at the promise of your return.

With streams of milk and hazelnut,
getting lost in tangled roots of coffee bean hair,
I stretch, my legs painted with the reddening sun.
I quite like breaking the dawn with you.

CORNERS

A roll.
A sigh.
A smile.

Folded pillows,
tangled sheets,
vodka aftermath,
and buttermilk dreams.

Your hands,
my stomach,
a soothing touch.

The world is fraught
with chaos,
such an imperfect place;
yet two people
have the magnitude
to still the storms
and piece perfect corners
in a world
that spins in circles.

KNOTTED BRANCHES

Whenever I play that song,
I can taste our summer on the tip of my tongue.
Like sungrown nectar, it ripples sweetness
across the roof of my mouth.

It is no longer a distant memory, but one that loops
like the 90 passing suns
in front of my film reel lashes.
I see porch light stars and know the beauty in
salt and sweat on skin under crescent moons.

Letting it burrow into your marrow and giving
yourself wholly to another until
our veins run with melted colors of
vibrancy and zealous infernos.

I smell the incense burn into the wrinkles
of my cotton tank top and fade into
midnight eyes, knowing that 3 a.m. marks the time
you stir each night to light
those wicks that feed us smoke
and leave my senses howling.

I am one with the knotted branches in my stomach –
the twists and dances that they do only to birth
such ardent wildflowers.
Every time the bass echoes, I recall how
every nerve in my body stood erect
like burning blue flames.
And the butterflies,
much like my love for you,
have yet to fly away.

PROTECTOR

I recall watching her walk into a room –
poetic, strong, stoic – like slightly thawed ice water.
She is woven out of sacrifice and wicker chair knotted wires of gold.
The hallmark of a topaz kind of love.
She lives in pocket kept dreams and underbelly streams,
and strokes wisps behind ears and heals last night's leftover pains.
She is a blue lace kind of gentle; a lioness protector.
I see myself in her eyes, her tears, her delicate hands.
I spend countless hours dancing in fireside rings as she
spins cotton dresses and angel white necklaces.
I smell Sundays of blueberry muffin batter and breeze blown windows,
and choose to inhale her goodness in our granite-covered kitchen.
She is a goddess of motherhood and soothes like tender chamomile.
She molds my Play-Doh dreams into brick houses that arch to the sky.
and with her hand holding mine, we build bridges of full lives
Of coral and copper sands, where she teaches me of womanhood and
wild independence like only the fiercest mother can.

SACCHARINE SAILOR

I long for freedom, she said.
To stretch sea foam arms and bite sea salt lips.
Motherly waves, won't you carry me home?

Poor, landlocked sailor, she only desires to
leave the city lights in the direction her hair blows.

Let me disavow my anchors, and set forth on
wooden pleats of cherry and oak.
I will stumble with the rising tide and cure
my wanderlust eyes that yearn to dance with the
Northern lights and the pirouette of Polaris.

She pockets Rose Quartz and trusts the Universe
to nourish her blistered soul.
With sapphire eyes, she leaves footprints in mounds
of dirt, following the light of seraphim out to
where the shore tickles her blushing toes.

With city candles that flicker on hillsides, I set my
eyes to the ink of the sea and my head to the
wolfish moon that is howling independence.
I leave the time of mud and mountains, and sway with
hollow air and distant sirens. My arms rise in
Braille bumps, but then, then Mother Moon wails:

My saccharine sailor, strength is bred from the heart,
not the flesh.

ICARA

She wanted to experience true beauty
under the sun and snow,
beneath the awning of winter.
She craved the warmth of
another's knuckles grazing hers.

Only curiosity could hold her –
she was far too exotic
for anything of this ordinary world,
like Saigon cinnamon and cardamom,
she was gentle and airy,
longing for a nomad to live with her
among the pinnacles and pines,
to rid her of the loneliness
that filled her hazel eyes.

She felt the soul of the Earth
pulse beneath her bare feet,
her toes tickling the dirt with wonder.
She ached for the heavens above,
a drunken sky filled with a
medley of colors –
nirvana's confetti.

It had to be said;
she believed true beauty was
above her and below her –
she wanted to feel it within her.

A fellow journeyer that could build her
wings that would let her
be one with the Earth,
be one with the heavens.

She longed to be Icarus,
taken by the sun,
cracked frost melted,
lifted through a canopy of trees.

She was gentle, airy –
beautiful
as the heavens and Earth,
a gypsy's heart,
a lonely soul.

With misty eyes,
she went up in flames,
burning – blending with the drunken sky,
her tears rained down
as she finally realized:

She never needed another's touch,
for with her own two hands,
she could build wings,
and set herself free.

THE STORYTELLER

I am a collector of books. Perhaps I am not a poet, but a storyteller. I am a reader. The works of those that have come before me know far more than that brain of mine that longs to be satiated. I lust for life and prose and words and literature. They fill my bones with myth and magic. They embed themselves in my nomadic mind.

I am a traveler. I long to climb over cerulean mountains, blister my toes among cobblestone paths of ginger and auburn sand, and let the tides hold me in a welcome home sea.

It is through novels and my rambling feet that I can experience far more lives than the one I have been granted. Dear humans, we used to be so free. We used to wander and wonder – when did we allow four walls to trick us into believing we are home? We have the key to set ourselves free from a prison fraught with familiarity and certainty. We must be okay with turning brass doorknobs and breaking our knotted roots. We must be okay with leaving.

But my beloved, you ask me why?

Because I am wild like lightning that can bend trees to its will. There is so much that will be left unanswered, darling. And I simply can't have that. I won't have that. I was made to run with wolves and paint the stones of caves red with wonder.

I am not an archetype, I will not be anonymous; I am ageless, passionate, and filled with such natural fury that when I leave this place, the lands I have wandered across will take me in and plant my soul in a fantasy I made my reality.

Let me grow my hair long; let it tangle in the wind, for what is humanity if not wild chaos?

Because the true question is, love, ***why not?***

EXPLORER

We are explorers.
We walk among the ruins of faded cobblestones
and the histories of past rains and riots.
Through desert plants and potted jewels
of rubies and emerald leaves.
Sweet summer cherries and tea kettle dreams,
we remain nimble through winding staircases
and softly spun songs.
Our footsteps splash in running rivers
and trace our initials in stardust and ash.
We were made to move. To run. To wander.
To question how deep our roots go
and to where they intertwine.
For what good is this life if we live standing still?
Hands steadied on rusted railings, we mold
copper statues with twine and twigs.
Our pilgrimage is eternal.
We dig deep, fumbling through this world with
grace, gratitude, and an ever growing need for adventure.

HOME

They say home is where the heart is.

I think I will make my home in the backbone
of damp soil, misty with river reflections
and carmine bricks.

Stacked in the heart of a coral valley, I will
spend my mornings brewing Nantucket coffee
grounds, stirring in a tad too much sugar.
Because when have any of us actually
overdosed on sweetness?

Brown, not white.
I love the way brown sugar crystallizes.
Like a Connecticut sun on autumn leaves.

Where I can see the moon tremble as it rises
against a star-speckled canvas draped in
calligraphy ink.

And as the clock strikes 12, a magnetic midnight
will be chimed in by the Roman goddess that
lights up the darkness with cosmic rays to
unveil the divinity of the Aurora Borealis.

I will call Mother Earth my parent, and nurse
a Sylvia Plath stove back to health.
Practical enough to flip blueberry pancakes and
burn batter-basted fingers.

On a strip of land that is one with an apricot sky,
this is where my heart lies.

REBIRTH

Beneath my boulder fortress, I emerge from hiding.

I peel away flayers of decaying flesh from the woman I once was to reveal someone wild, unbroken. Unyielding.

No longer a girl, I dive into the synapses of my mind and inhale scents of paprika and thyme, concocting midnight potions and spellbound scrolls.

My soul has ripened into a golden age; my spirit remains timeless as that stilled pocket watch that hangs from my windowsill.

Hands that hold at 12:01 – the breaking of a new day; an opportunity to improve and follow the sea until the shoreline evaporates into its indigo lips.

I am no longer afraid of the mysteries of this world; I welcome it into my arms as a mother to her child.

I know longer keep thoughts behind locked cabinets; I sprinkle them across laddered shelves and sew them into words of cascading confidence and earthly strength.

The monsters have been kept at bay – they cling to rocks for fear of the underworld.

For fear of what lies beneath the corpse of this prior woman.

Now I run through Niagara orchards and meadows of ginger poppies that roam as free as legged creatures.

I have traveled, realm to realm, overturning new destinies and fighting fate's condemnation.

No, not even fate can beat the ferocity out of me. Out of us.

I run with packs of reckless stallions and sweat from the womb of the unknown.

The past will not define me.

I have collected enough pebbles, gems, and heavy memories to break the window of freedom.

And now I know more than ever, I am reborn.

WILD HEAVEN

I keep my head in the stars.
I want to hear my voice echo against the dying sun
and the twinkling moon.
Caress fireflies and lightning bugs and soar
on a supernova.
Bend the cosmos to reflect rainbow light and
magnetic prisms to another dimension.
Carry me away on Orion's belt and let me slow dance
on the rings of Saturn, melting ice like whiskey fire.
They can have my insecurities, the flaws,
the darkness that the sky's soul holds.
I am building pyramids above the horizon – some sort
of eternity that will hold time still and guide
the hands of ticking tower clocks to Neverland.

Maybe it will never be enough.
Maybe because I can never possibly get enough.
I want wild herds of comets and asteroids,
an anchor to Venus and the lakes of Mars.
Bring me to the shorelines of the universe,
the fringe of forever.
For I do not need wings to fly.
I will crawl inside of a cannon;
shoot me up somewhere near wild heaven.

THE COUNTDOWN

(One, two, three).

It has been said that the Big Bang only lasted three seconds before the fall of stasis. It is rather easy to fall prey to the sky's expanse. Looking way, way up, and way, way back. Hydrogen atoms, gravity – 300 million years. Slow clumps of molasses caramelizing among the gray matter of the universe. Playing hopscotch through the periodic table. Forming stars from helium and light. White dwarfs, red giants. Nuclear fusion and supernovas. It is rather easy to see the world even in the dark. We are curious scientists and falling astronauts that see the stars for what they once were.

It has been said that we are primarily made of stardust. Perhaps it is hydrogen and water. Maybe we are all three. Beating in the hearts of stars and scattering our particles across the globe. Through sapphire oceans and emerald islands. Rock candy caves and confectionary comets that streak the sky like mile-high lanterns.

We are dazzling sparks of glitter, shimmering in graphs of cityscapes and power lines. Dizzy with wonder, filling beakers with smoky potions and bottling light years to steal time. Blurry beasts that rush through the path of planets. Zodiac signs align over the realm of the sun, eclipsing constellations and waltzing with Hyakutake's Comet. How quick they come and go. How chaotic they burst into the sky's wilderness. Like them, we long to shake the land and create new dimensions – we long to be the best versions of ourselves. Astronauts that see the stars for what they once were. Time travelers that are stuck in the past, collecting neon love like old ships in nautical bottles and varnishing ourselves in the chalk dust of hopscotch lines.

But it has been said that we are primarily made of stardust. So if that is true, then even we at (four, five, six, and seven) feet can build a galaxy. Sand castle pyramids. Lighting bolts of Zeus. Mother's milk painted throughout Andromeda. We will rage. Burn. Spread spiral fires and inhale phoenix ash. We are just like the stars. Mortal. A burst of atomic light, quick to change with the ebb and flow. And even in their dying moment, they shine ever so brightly.

(Three, two, one).

PHOENIX RISING

To the little girl that didn't belong,

I am here to tell you that it gets better.

You would rather fold origami cranes than play tetherball. So what?
And you'd watch kids point at you with their index fingers while you used yours to push your glasses up so they would actually sit atop your nose. It's okay that your jeans were a tad too short. You spoke in mellifluous tones, and perhaps it was this epoch in time that hit you hardest.

Yes, I know serendipity was not a kind friend to you. With Lisa Frank stickers and a tangled head of chocolate string, I know you sat on those green benches wondering if and where you could find your place in the world. Maybe it was alongside the knotted knuckles of that old oak tree at the bottom of the schoolyard? Where you could lie supine and gaze at a firecracker sky, wondering if such a thing as sunkissed moonbeams could actually exist, or was that, too, just another paradox?

I know you longed to roam the moon and bathe in stardust, but because you couldn't fly like your cranes, you took to your spiral bound notebook to write squiggly letters in iridescent ink. *Once upon a time...* Or didn't it go something like that?

You lived in fantasies, and had an imaginary friend. You had real friends, too, but they would rather collect Polly Pockets than calligraphy sets.

And you, you precious girl, I am so sorry that no one was stronger for you. That you spent your childhood terrified of a man you should have trusted. That when you were alone with him, I know you held onto some scintilla of hope that after ten minutes, it would all be over. *Just hang on, firecracker eyes...*

I know in those moments the place you longed to be most was hidden inside a crater of that celestial crescent, propelling your rocket ship with pinwheel hands and guided by paper mâché lanterns and sparkler stars.

Little one, do not fear anymore. Emerge from your labyrinth and take a look at that halcyon sun. You do not have to spend your time dancing with silhouettes, nor cowering in his presence. You will find others like you. And you will build cities of land and sky, and fall in love with another landlocked astronaut and he too, is looking for a place to call home.

You do not need a rocket ship. You have wings. Fly, phoenix, fly.

To the little girl that didn't belong –

I am here to tell you that it gets better.

I am here to tell you that it *got* better.

Love always,
Sam

PHOENIX FINISH

I have far too many ideas.

Unfiltered and clamoring for release like caged lovebirds seeking a couple's reprieve.

I run with wolves and sleep in the copper caves of wild beasts that roam pinecone corners of an unbroken Earth.

Beneath the catacombs and ancient carnivals, I know there must be more.

I know we can be more.

We must be.

Got to be.

Have to be.

Grow like wild strawberry vines and carry messages into the dawn.

I light amber incense and let the ash burn into the tabletop.

Because I need to remind myself that every molecule is mortal.

That to inhale and exhale is a precious privilege.

Not a right.

And I'll tell children to *rage against the dying of the light.*

I clap almond flour into the air,

watch the powder fall,

dust my wooden floor canvas, let my arms sprawl,

angel wings, angel cake batter,

I live out art with every starflake and starburst.

Each soul stirring moment.

I fear it might not be enough,

I fear the sound of sirens,

so I light coal on fire and burn out diamonds.

I write, I ignite, I will not let my flame be diminished.

I have far too many ideas.

So I will rise again – an endless finale, my phoenix finish.

www.ingramcontent.com/pod-product-compliance
Lightning Source LLC
Chambersburg PA
CBHW071838020426
42331CB00007B/1780